The Best of

COW

TIPPING

PRESS

VOLUME 1

Introduction
by Zeena Fuleihan

"I guess there's all different kinds of beautiful.
Very
well. Different kinds of love.
Know the concept. The vocabulary."

—Dar Cieminski, "The Hippie Chick"

Sometimes, it may seem like language is the glue that holds the human population together. Students frantically study verb conjugations in their foreign language classes, parents attempt to keep up with their teenagers' lingo, lawyers settle cases over punctuation marks. And yet, the best writing almost always breaks "the rules." Poetry mesmerizes because it evokes emotion without instructions; instead it eludes fixed definition and elicits splendor in its ability to use vocabulary in new ways.

Despite our obsession with grammar and denotations, we can communicate without standard speech. We can learn someone's body language and facial expressions, identify emotion through the rhythm or pitch of their words instead of the meaning. Read between the lines.

Dar Cieminski writes, "Vocabulary / is a big concept of poetic words of a dictionary that / you / make up."

Language has infinite meanings and communication can be accomplished in infinite ways. Something may make sense to one person and not the next, but through rephrasing, both learn to understand it in a different light.

Our vocabulary is never stable, always adapting to new concepts. Sometimes, it needs a push to step outside of what it knows.

Through creative writing classes and published books, Cow Tipping Press creates a platform for adults with developmental disabilities to speak for themselves and share their vocabularies, revealing a few more of communication's myriad pathways. This anthology samples just some of the incredible pieces by Cow Tipping authors from its first ten volumes. I hope it helps you expand your own vocabulary, and shows you that

"Beautiful
can be almost any word."

Survival
by Brad Kellar

I think hunger is important, a hunger for life. And that no one can tell you how to live your life. You should be able to live it the way you want to. Appetite would be something to eat. Appetite would be, you know, after you've eaten a lot of food, that you wouldn't want to go and eat something else. That your appetite is good enough. Appetite for something to drink, like milk or juice or water. I think hunger is the wilderness. The animals. Life. Hunger for something exciting to happen. Hunger for something—how can I put it? Hunger for being alive. Hunger for being brave. Hunger for exploring. Hunger for nature. Hunger for the sounds. Hunger for creation. Hunger for beauty. Hunger for not knowing what's coming. Hunger for creating something. Hunger for being who you are. Hunger would be sound, different kinds of sounds. Hunger would be the stars, the moon, the sun. Hunger would be creation.

Childhood Themes
by Dar Cieminski

A police dog, I don't know what the name of the police dog is. Let's call him Shepherd. He's surviving a gunshot. He got shot in the head. It's not very nice. It's going to take a little time for him to recover, but I'd like to hear more stories about good things. I like the movie *Free Willy 1, 2,* and *3.* I guess you could say childhood themes, with the mother with the broken dorsal. That was a true story. I think it's important that people keep their violence to a minimum and start a revolution and find the right answer. I'd like to see more of the raptor centers for the wounded animals. I'd like to see more adopted dogs, cats. Generally, good things like art and music help soothe the boredom. We know about the bad, we know about the good, what about the revolutionary?

Beach Boys
by Barb Rabe

How about history. And how about think about history. How about shadow. How about think about shadow. How about think about listen to a poem. How about thinking about a poem. How about Beach Boys. How about having a person.

Your Mind
by Vince Fiorilli

Some minds are dark
But minds can be bright
I just heard a tone that makes you glad
But what does it do
makes you happy and open your mind to do
something fun
oh my, oh my, oh my
let's open our mind and have fun

Oranges
by Denise Cady

It is a fruit. Need to be peeled and cut and other fruit need to be cut and other fruit need to be cut up. Watermelon, blueberry, raspberry, berry cantaloupe, blackberry. Everything is juice.

You Should Go to the Fair So You Won't Get Bored and Be a Bum Around the House All Day
by Josh Gertz

The fair can be a lot of fun. Sometimes they have games there. It gives you something to do, to walk around. Sometimes they have food there. Sometimes they have pizza there. Sometimes you can look around. Sometimes they have animals there. Sometimes they have the little guinea pheasants there. They can chase you around. You should duck down like a brick to get them to stop chasing. Take your time while you're ducking down. Slow down and be patient while you're doing it. You should look behind you before you make your move. They start small before they grow up. Sometimes they can pluck you like a real hammer and then you can bail out and get out of sight. It really helps if you leave them alone for a whole year. They don't have to do this to you. If you leave them alone, basically they'll leave you alone. Sometimes they like to run. Sometimes they make these weird noises.

Sometimes they have chickens at the fair. You can look at

them, but don't try to touch them or jump on them. They can eat you. They sure can. Just don't even try to do anything with them. At the fair you can walk around, but you've got to keep your hands to yourself. Just don't even try to do anything with them at all. They can pluck out your hair and use it as a love nest. You can look around. That's fine. You sure can. The fair here in town is a free fair. They finally changed the sign. You can go on rides if you pay attention to what you're doing so you won't get hurt. You need to look both ways where you're going. Sometimes they have mini donuts there. You can eat them anytime you feel like it, just in case you have nothing better for food at your home. Sometimes you can look at the rides to see how they run. You should go to the fair so you won't get bored and be a bum around the house all day. That's why we have to have fairs.

Ode to Drawings
by Benny Sheaks

Sketch Pad: I draw those pictures;
pictures of waving hands, picture of "WELCOME TO"
words, picture of
"GREETINGS" words, picture of "ONCE"
words, picture of "TWICE" words, pictures
of letters of the alphabet, pictures of counting the
numbers, pictures of colors,
pictures of shapes, pictures of solid shapes,
pictures of rhymes, pictures of
Nursery Rhymes, picture

on *"*Ode to Drawings*"*
by Rachel Lieberman

In "Ode to Drawings," Benny Sheaks celebrates both the
sketchpad and the act of drawing. Sheaks expresses
intense enthusiasm through the use of capitalization and
punctuation. Using only commas to separate the phrases,
he creates a sense of crescendo, giving weight to each
phrase yet prohibiting the reader from pausing too long
before continuing, and asking for the whole ode to be
given in one breath. By capitalizing "WELCOME TO,"
"GREETINGS," "ONCE," and "TWICE," and putting the words
in quotations, Sheaks demands special attention be given
to the magnificence of the images. The first line of the
poem, "Sketch Pad: I draw those pictures;" conjures both
the product and the act of drawing. The poem glorifies
the images, but perhaps more importantly glorifies the
excitement and pride that stems from the creation and
ownership of art.

While Sheaks's visual imagery is strong and specific (for

example the word "GREETINGS"), he leaves some images more open to the reader's interpretation. Toward the end of the poem, he describes more vague and fantastical images (for example, "pictures of rhymes") and then continues to give more context to shape the reader's conceptualization, writing, "pictures of Nursery Rhymes." Familiar and simple images from childhood like nursery rhymes, shapes, and counting the numbers may evoke nostalgia in the reader. The combination of nostalgia and the increasingly open-ended imagery leads into Sheaks's final, seemingly unfinished and unpunctuated statement, "picture" (is it a noun or verb?). The crescendo of the poem trails off, as if lost in the memories of drawing and drawings, or speculation about all the possible images one could draw.

Advice to Daughter
by Thomas Robinson

Be nice to people. Don't be mean to people. Be nice to your elders. Be nice to people with disabilities. Be an advocate for yourself. Always be on time. Sometimes be late. Always hold your hand when you cross the street. Don't jaywalk. Don't hurt other people. Don't hurt yourself. Be positive. Don't let the evil beast destroy you.

Ode to Tomatoes and Potato
by Sarah Debbins

Which is which
Tomatoes is vegetable
How old is tomatoes
Tom always has atoes
Just like cat named Tom
ate cat food into mashed
Potatoes with tiptoe in
the kitchen opened
refrigerator get a
Tator Tots out of freezer
to make cat food into
Tomatoes mixed with
Potatoes into Pot of
Tom Tator toes hot dish

The Overprotective Mom
by Ethan Bussiere

Mothers can be overprotective. My opinion is that if you can't allow someone a chance to be fully independent—well, how do you know they can't? Some parents think it is being hard to let go. They think that when we stumble they have to be there to catch us, but if we always had a safety net then we could never build the blocks back together again, like an independent person would have to. So how do you become something you're never allowed to try? It's like going to dance lessons and being stopped at the door. You'll never learn to dance if you can't put your feet on the floor. So all in all, parents should let disabilitied children a chance to try to be independent before they put up the roadblock. They may be surprised at the results.

When You're Gone
by Shinoa Makinen

When you're gone, life will leave us. We all fly from the sky. We are the wind, the breeze. If I go one day, don't cry for me. I am not there, you see. I didn't die. I am the uplift rush. I am the ash and dust. If I had to live my life, I live it until my death. So when I am gone don't call me on phone. I won't be there to answer. I am the soul that lives in air. I am the glint in the snow. I am free. I am the touch of little feet. I am a child of thee.

The Hippie Chick
by Dar Cieminski

Thanks
for the comment. Thank you.
I guess there's all different kinds of beautiful.
Very
well. Different kinds of love.
Know the concept. The vocabulary.

Vocabulary
is more like a sentence full of poetic words. Thank
you. Love
for your pet. A sheep is a ewe.
Very well.
Flowers are beautiful.

Flower magic. I look beautiful.
I want a big vocabulary.
I look very
nice. Thank
you.
Love

me. I love
thee. I count the ways. I look beautiful.
You
are my best friend. Vocabularic
poetry. Thanks
a lot. I thank you very

much. The very
end. Hippie chick love.
I thank
you. I look beautiful.
Vocabulary
is a big concept of poetic words of a dictionary that you

make up. You
love me. Very very.
Vocabulary.
It's just a bunch of words that you put together in

a sentence. Love me love you love myself. Love
your pet. Love your mom and dad. Love your sisters,
brothers. Love your teacher. Love the help. Love your staff.
Beautiful
can be almost any word. Thank

you. You can. Very
good. Vocabulary words. Love
you. Beautiful me. Thank you.

Freedom
by Lyn Johnson

I'm 63 years old. I'll be 64 next year. I'm a good worker at Valley Natural Foods. And I'm still single. I have a boyfriend and he's slow getting me an engagement ring. He always says that, "Let's get married, let's get married." And I say, "When?" I'll be 90 years old by the time I get married! I'm still looking for an apartment. I gotta get out of that group home—it's getting worse ever. I lost my mom, my dad, and my brother. My dad had been drinking and got himself drunk. That's why I'm trying to tell people stop drinking and stop smoking. And I don't have contact with the rest of my family. That's myself.

I tell people, smoking causes cancer. I wish people would quit drinking and driving and get themselves in trouble. Because my dad got drunk at the bar after work and he hit the telephone pole. I got after him. And my mom started getting after him. I said, "Mom, you don't know what he's doing." And he hit the telephone pole.

Every once a weekend I go see my mom and dad's grave. I'm going to see them again, because I'm going to be buried there if something happens to me. I want to see my brother's graveyard too, next time. Because I do miss my mom, my dad, and my brother. I remember, I don't have no grandparents any more. I just got nieces and nephews, but I don't hear from them. Hopefully, through this day I'm going to keep on working till I'm retired. I've got so many jobs—I retired so many jobs. Didn't work out. I pray the God to help me out. I go to church every Sunday. That's about it.

Gratitude to Plants
by Bruce Zentic

It's like the plants need rain and sun, then they'll grow. Feeding the plants after it gets some sun, it'll grow. Then it will grow. When the fall comes the leaves will turn and it'll all fall out. In the winter they die off, then the plants are all dead. The plants they would stay alive, they wouldn't die out and plants never grow lilacs like the purple. Only the trees, bushes. And I know trees grow leaves. Small leaves and big leaves. And dandelions come from—they used to remind me, 'cause they're like yellow, remind me of butter. Dandelions, dandelions, what's in them? Why they're yellow? Sunflower, sunflower.

High School Musical 2
by Amanda Woolley

Killed. A mask. Spy movies. And then he got hit in the nose with a gun. Oh, the police too. Like the movies. He got away in a raft outside. He was tied to a chair and was killed too. Following is a spy. And the DVD, and good. Guy was in the house, with a mask. Was stealing a book. That's it. They did a good job. Oh, the snow. Yeah, snow was with the spy in the winter. Sunny in the sky. And a person was killed, tied to the chair.

The Fall
by Robert Bergerson

The jazz music sounds like going to a restaurant, like any old restaurant. Like even when you go to sports places. My brother-in-law is in a band that plays jazz music. When I hear that music, I think it sounds like a river flowing down the street. It makes me want to dance. I think of the seasons. Like falling leaves when I hear the music playing.

The Breakfast
by Dar Cieminski

the / breakfast table
the / most memorable food
waffles / w choc chips
and / scramble / eggs and sausage
w / spices and cheese / writing
on my Kindle Fire hd 6
poem at breakfast table

A Good Cup of Coffee
by Denise Cieminski

CoffeeGood,
WATERCREAM
HOTINCUP!

A Granddaughter's Farewell to Her Grandpa
by Shinoa Makinen

A young girl six years old. Her grandpa first brought her up north, a three-hour drive away where there crops on the farming field. In the country, out of town, Menahga, MN. He lived his life. He loved the countryside. He loved the dirt on the road where he rides his four-wheeling tricks for fun. He loves to cook and bake sometimes. He is the country living years where he wakes up at dawn, hear the rooster crows cooks eggs from my cousin's farm next door works all day until sun goes down. He loves to be fishing on a boat and sleep in the camper with grandchildren. He loves roasting marshmallow and make s'more on a campfire everytime. He is the country living year where he rides his orange Corvette to anyplace. He wear hats all the time. A three-hour drive away where he served the peace. He loved the country, out of town, Menahga, MN. My grandpa lived in the trailer house. He loves the countryside all the time. A young girl six years old. Her grandpa brought her up north where there's tree plants animal on the farming field. He is the country living life. In the country, out of town, Menahga, MN. He lived his life on a farm. He worked on construct stuff before he served for peace. He loved a three-hour drive away where it's quiet each day. Two days before he passed away another left to sleep at rest, on July 3rd at 4 PM 2016. The Lord called my grandpa to rest in peace in the country, out of town, Menahga, MN. My grandpa lived his life on a farm, a three-hour drive away where it quiet since he left that summer day. In the country, out of town, Menahga, MN. My grandpa built the trailer house, helped so many on the way before he served the armed force for peace for freedom of liberty. A three-hour drive away, where there woods trees animals and crops on the farming field in the country. Out of town. Menahga, MN. He lived in the trailer house. He is the country living life.

What a Tiger Can Do
by Vince Fiorilli

My oh my, what can a tiger do
If you believe in a tiger
they can make you brave and unstoppable
they also can make you smart and wise
you can even make a good guard
but the question is, do you want all that?
I'd say just do things your way, not the tiger way

The Wright Brothers and the Crazy Horses
by Jay Boyce

The flying Wright brothers jumped out of a barracuda. The Wright brothers said, "Don't eat us. We're too big for you." Then the sweet little dust bunny asked the barracuda to spit out the Wright brothers. The barracuda was busy trying to swim and eat plankton. Then the Wright brothers saved the barracuda and crab for lunch. The Wright brothers decided to eat fish. Then they jumped over the meadow and saw a couple of crazy horses jumping out of the lamp. The barracuda was trying to invent a sugar cookie that was so hard, like a rock. The Wright brothers saw a cute little star. Then they saw a couple of bunnies jumping out of a crazy horse. Then they saw a little birdie. The little birdie was hopping on the bunny trail. The bunnies asked the Wright brothers, "Which way are we going? Are we going east, south, or west?"

Enjoy the Moment
by Daniel Weldin

See rain feels
Like freezing, tastes
Like rain drops
Smells like umbrella

What Advice Meant to Me
by Sarah Debbins

I would like to give some advice to my guardians, my house
staff, and to Lifeworks staff. I have problems with stealing
or lying, especially telling the truth given advice from my
therapists and counselors, to help me find the answer my
questions about my own problems on my meds throughout
my depressions and let my anger out with my OCD and
Down Syndrome to really cut down on paxil meds, because
my body usually gave me headache, dizzy spells and nerves
breakdown, but I need more help giving more advice, it
really help me in God's prayer for hope turned it around to
have faith in me to be strong and very last. "I can do it, just
do it."

Story of Advice by Sarah Debbins

The Authors

Robert Bergerson is a great poet, a very good poet. He likes to say what's on his mind. It's like enjoying life every day. He is the winner of the University of Minnesota's Stephanie Award for his piece "The Fall."

Jay Boyce has a nice family. He wants to work at Best Buy.

Ethan Bussiere loves to write fantasy short stories. He also likes to write poems and lyrics. He feels his writing comes from his vast imagination. He can't keep his mind quiet, so why not write it?

Denise Cady takes Metro Mobility. She goes to church. She goes on Monday and Wednesday to Community Culture Center. She goes to her brother for supper and movie night. She also does choir and spends time with her family and friend Kristen. Saturdays are open.

Dar Cieminski likes to write poetry. She's from Minneapolis. She's in a group home. She likes to write. Free will.

Denise Cieminski is a very nice person. She has a nice family. She has a friend named Kurt. Not Kurt Vonnegut. Her friend's name is Kurt Gowell.

For her life, **Sarah Debbins** spends time with staff one-on-one outing and going on date outing with her boyfriend Roger with assistant staff. She does a lot spending her bedroom to research on computers, taking notes, finger typing and get along with her roommates with her staff doing movies and snack night or TV shows.

Vince Fiorilli had many dreams in his life. He even had so many dreams he didn't know where to start. After a while all that was left was writing. And man does he get compliments on what he writes and his imagination.

Josh Gertz is a good person because he likes to be around people. He likes to talk a lot with his friends. He is a very good friend.

Brad Kellar is 59 years old and was born in 1956. He does not know what hospital he was born in. His dad was an alcoholic and it was very hard to live at home when he was drinking. His mom and her friend were aged two years apart and she started drinking as well. How did he put up with it? His mom said he had to be strong. When his sisters and his brother moved out he was all alone. When he lived on his own he would go buy a pack of beer and that was a tough time in his life. He found out that he had a lot of support in his life and people that loved him.

Lyn Johnson is still single. Oh boy, now she'll probably get more boyfriends on her. She just wants one, not a bunch.

Shinoa Makinen started writing 2008. She enjoys knitting. She goes to choir and she write songs from her heart. She has an aunt who is a piano teacher. She enjoys her music instrument flute.

Barb Rabe likes to color. She likes to get better. She likes to work hard.

Thomas Robinson is from Minneapolis. He lives in Bloomington. He has a twin brother. He likes to draw. He's a self-advocate. He likes writing about anything and everything.

Benny Sheaks likes to draw and do crafts. He's drawing a picture of Independence Day. Draw those pictures of Martin Luther King Day two times. Turkey and birdhouse crafts. Bowling. Five strikes. And then those pictures of Hanukah. And then those pictures of Christmas Eve. And then those pictures of Kwanzaa. And then those pictures of New Years' Day.

Daniel Weldin loves playing basketball and riding bikes with Bethany. He likes writing about basketball too. He sings, dances, and drinks chocolate milk. Green is his favorite color.

Amanda Woolley reads books. And movies. Rainbow books. Three Little Pigs. And a camp. Bears.

Bruce Zentic is from Minneapolis. He likes old cars and phonographs, stereos and radios. He likes writing about certain stuff that grows, like lilacs. He likes dandelions like butter. He still likes his cucumber pickles. He likes lights and "go" signs. He likes riding a bike.

Made in the USA
Monee, IL
28 January 2022